OPERATIN
ABUNDANCE

GET READY TO OPEN THE DOORWAY TO DIVINE MYSTERY
THROUGH **THE 23RD PSALM**

ADONIJAH O. OGBONNAYA, PH.D.

אתה

OPERATING IN ABUNDANCE
Adonijah O. Ogbonnaya, Ph.D.
Second Edition

Publications Copyright © 2009, literature arm of AACTEV8 International
(Apostolic Activation Network)
Aactev8 International 1020 Victoria Ave. Venice, CA 90291

www.aactev8.com

Published by Seraph Creative 2022
ISBN: 978-1-958997-10-9

Edited by Kathy Strecker & Jonathan Brown

Library of Congress data

Alchemy, prayer, provisions, personal growth, spirituality. The Lord's Prayer, Will, will of man, will of God, Kingdom of God, heaven, forgiveness, temptation, spiritual power, transformation, Bible study.

No part of this book may be reproduced, stored in retrieval system, or transmitted in any form or by any means, electronic, mechanical, photocopy, recording or otherwise except for brief quotation in print review without prior permission from the holder of the copyright.

Scripture quotations from the New American Standard Bible, unless otherwise stated. ESV, NIV, NKJV, KJV

Cover art by Feline Graphics

Typesetting, Illustration & Layout by Feline
www.felinegraphics.com

אתה

CONTENTS

5	FOREWORD
6	HOW TO READ THIS BOOK
7	PRAYER
9	CHAPTER 1 *Our Ever-Present Provider*
15	CHAPTER 2 *In Green Pastures*
21	CHAPTER 3 *Paths of Righteousness*
29	CHAPTER 4 *Walking in the Shadow*
37	CHAPTER 5 *God's Table*
43	CHAPTER 6 *Head, Hands and Feet*
53	CHAPTER 7 *Psalm 23*
64	APPENDIX A: THE HEBREW ALEPH BET
65	ABOUT THE AUTHOR
66	ABOUT SERAPH CREATIVE

אתה

אתה

FOREWORD

When I first preached these messages at our local church in Venice, God promised me that He would show people the heart of abundance as I was preaching, and that our community, and my global family would move into a greater level of abundance.

Let me say, this book is not just about money, or finances, or even just about business, this book is written to help you become a person of generosity. As I complete this book, I stand in awe of God's divine plan, in the midst of the Covid-19 pandemic when the earth moved to a place of fear and lack.

As I release this revelation, I trust that God will move in your life, to change the operating system of your life, this book enables the believer to walk on the path of abundance, being a person of wealth, in every area of life.

I used the template of Psalm 23, a well-known scripture in the eyes of many, however allow me to illuminate your path again, as God has shone His divine light when revealing the hidden mysteries of this scripture to me.

I believe this book will provide you with keys to freedom, keys that will be with you for the rest of your life, as David, the friend of God, learned the ways of God, so you can walk in those same paths, into a place where the living water of God never runs out in every area of your life.

We serve a God who has given to us abundantly, His only Son, Jesus Christ, not just the Saviour of the world, but a gift from a Father to His children, saying to humanity, I value you more than gold, and silver, I value you more than my creation, I can only show you my love by sending my Son, to show you the very heart of generosity.

I pray that God will bless you, as you learn the ways of righteousness in this book, may the Spirit of Wisdom impart to you, the wisdom to walk in ways that will bless your generations, and change the very frequency of your life, to joy, hope and a beautiful wonder and awe of the provision of God.

May God bless you and keep you.

Shalom
Dr Adonijah O. Ogbonnaya

אתה

HOW TO READ THIS BOOK

Psalm 23 is probably one of the most famous and well-loved bible passages of all time. To be sure, it's the psalm we first turn to as we cry out to our Father in times of need. Though this psalm is constantly at our fingertips, Dr. Ogbonnaya tells us that Psalm 23 contains significant truths and mysteries that we have not yet grasped nor appropriated into the way we relate to God and operate within His provision for us.

Operating in Abundance takes us on a journey to unlock the mysteries of Psalm 23 and enter a realm of discovery of the true essence of our Father's heart. Dr. Ogbonnaya meanders down the pathways that David himself traveled to help us encounter the nature of God and the length to which He goes to pursue us with His relentless love. Along the way, Dr. Ogbonnaya stops to unravel hidden levels of meaning and expounds on the significance of keywords and phrases, explaining how the Hebrew letters and the gematria enrich and support the deeper truths of God's goodness and mercy.

Come on this journey, armed with prayer and a spirit ready to demolish old paradigms and ways of thinking. Get ready to discover even more about our Father's goodness and tap into the endless possibilities of His eternal provision. There is a chart of the Aleph Bet at the end of the book to support you as Dr. Ogbonnaya breaks down certain words and phrases into their component parts in the Hebrew.

Get ready to open the door to His divine mysteries!

אתה

Psalm 23
King James Version (NASBKJV)

The Lord, *is* My Shepherd.
A Psalm of David.

¹The LORD *is* my shepherd; I shall not want.

²He maketh me to lie down in green pastures:
he leadeth me beside the still waters.

³He restoreth my soul: he leadeth me in the
paths of righteousness for his name's sake.

⁴Yea, though I walk through the valley of the shadow of death,
I will fear no evil: for thou *art* with me;
thy rod and thy staff they comfort me.

⁵Thou preparest a table before me in the presence of mine enemies:
thou anointest my head with oil; my cup runneth over.

⁶Surely goodness and mercy shall follow me all the days of my life:
and I will dwell in the house of the LORD for ever.

אתה

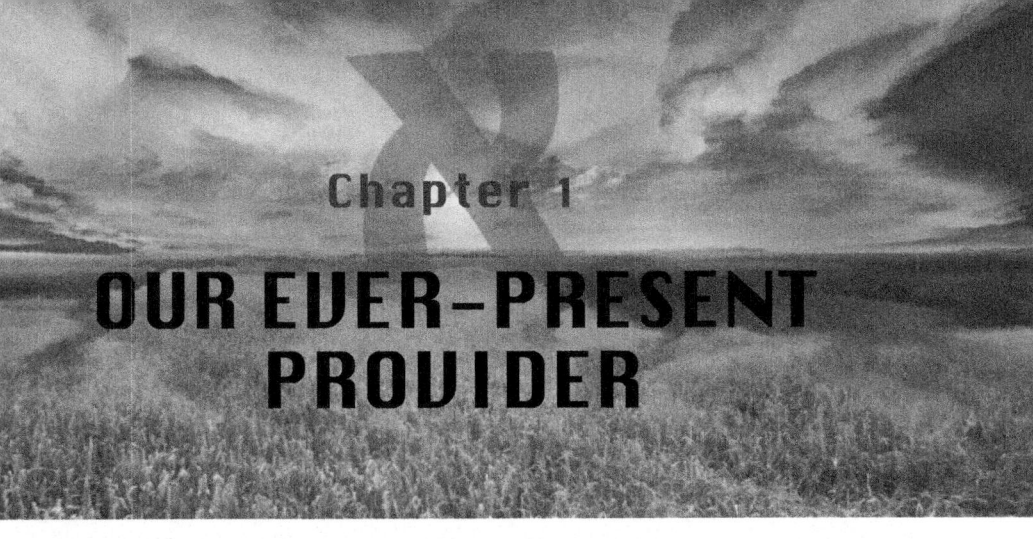

Chapter 1
OUR EVER-PRESENT PROVIDER

Human beings have been trained for millennia to believe that there is not enough, because of a place of lack. This is largely the basis for all wars and struggles—a belief of lack (I begin to look at some of the great wars that have been fought in the world.

The majority have been about economics). Many fears and anxieties derive from not having enough. Family quarrels are often centered around provision or the lack thereof. It seems that we have everything, yet we think we don't have enough. We are sold to the idea, in our psyche, that there is never enough. We think if we don't see it, then it is not there. In other words, our tendency to spiritualize and materialize lack ends up making us not understand anything beyond what we can see. Moreover, we have been taught that everything we have or has happened to us, we have worked for it. This is clearly untrue. Our thinking and beliefs are guided by many false assumptions around our understanding of provision.

After Moses led Israel out of Egypt and into the wilderness, they complained and asked for another God. If they were living in the wilderness sustained by God's provision, then why would Israel ask for another God? It is indicative of the intrinsic system and belief of lack to which they were accustomed and that God, himself, was not enough for them. They clamored for another god because they needed a god they could see, touch, and with whom to play. They needed a god less than themselves. When Israel entered the wilderness out of Egypt, they entered through a plethora of God's promises; they were God-led. God provided everything they needed in the wilderness. God

אתה

required nothing of them to bring them out of Egypt. They didn't create the lamb whose blood they used on the doorpost. The night of their supernatural deliverence, an angel forced the Egyptians to release them, even Israel was completely unaware of what happened that night. Everything that happened to them was a miracle of divine providence. God was fully present; however, because they had been trained to believe that there was never enough, even the presence of God was not enough.

What God performed in the miracle of the Red Sea is clear, if we understand it from the Jewish perspective. The bible says Israel went into the sea, indicating they were under water. And the sea parted, forming a wall on both sides. They had the sea above them and a sea wall on each side; they walked through a tunnel. This formation reveals the mystery of what God did: The water above and on each side formed the Hebrew letter "Heh". "Heh" represents a doorway to another dimension; thus, having entered the tunnel, Israel had entered another dimension.

> You could be suffering the same experience with another human being and, depending on your perspective, you will survive and they won't

The angel of God, who had been going before the camp of Israel, moved and went behind them; and the pillar of cloud moved from before them and stood behind them. So it came between the camp of Egypt and the camp of Israel; and there was the cloud along with the darkness, yet it gave light at night. Thus, the one did not come near the other all night (Exodus 14:19-20 NASB).

Many Jewish fathers' commentary about this miracle said by the combination of the Hebrew letters and the combination of the name of God, Moses was able to create angelic structure to stand the water up and in between them and the Egyptians. God was letting them know that they were in an eternal, infinite position. There was nothing that God could not become for them.

Israel emerged out of the tunnel—out of another dimension.

אתה

The tunnel brought them to the other side of the Red Sea with the Egyptian army far behind them. When Israel crossed to the other side, the scriptures say that God made the wheels of the Egyptians heavy, and there was darkness between Israel's side and the other side; consequently, the Egyptians could not cross to the other side. This further demonstrates that Israel had, in fact, entered another dimension. As coming out of the tunnel of water, Israel learned and understood that they could enter another dimension. This means that we can be in the same tunnel as others and, while their wheels get heavy, we move through easily. We could be suffering the same experiences that other humans suffer and, depending on our perspectives, we will survive and they won't. When Israel came out of the tunnel, they experienced provision at every turn because God did not change the process. He took the same angelic structure that existed in the water and placed it around them. We can see this in the darkness, the pillar of fire by night, and the pillar of cloud by day. It was the same process protecting them from whatever it was they were afraid of and what could have come against them. When they cried out, the same presence released provision—food or shelter. David said, "They ate the food of angels." Jesus said, "I am that bread in the wilderness." God wanted Israel to understand that they were slaves—a people who operate out of a position of lack— but they didn't have to worry about provision.

> If you operate from a place of lack, you can never be at rest. The answer to your restlessness could be to change the perspective about God's capacity to provide for you.

Lack is not simply about food, but everything that sustains our lives. If we start from lack, everyone around us is going to seem imperfect. We will never be satisfied with anything anyone does for us. God was communicating with Israel the principle of sufficiency or abundance—there is enough. If Israel would have understood the provision available to them, they would have been satisfied. If we understand that there is enough, then we can be satisfied. And if we are satisfied, we can love our brothers and sisters. We don't have to go to war against our spouses. Our idea of lack has been inexpedient. If we are not satisfied with what we have around us, we are constantly searching for something that isn't there; consequently, we will live

אתה

with a sense of emptiness, thinking we're not enough. Our world is informed by lack, which is fundamental to what we believe, think, and how we live. By living with a fundamental sense of lack, we create idols that are less than us to become our guardians.

Whenever we think there is not enough, we walk in fear and anxiety which forces us to think of people as things or objects. Without active self-examination, we cease to be human begins and think we're something that we are not. Our goal is not to be an angel, but to be human beings. We must examine why we behave toward others the way we do. Through self-examination, we understand that we need to repent, not that others need to repent. Making others repent is not our job; rather, we must rectify ourselves and keep ourselves in a position that allows us to see the way God is and how He relates to us. God does not relate to us in partiality and out of lack.

One reason we operate in a consciousness of lack is we fail to realize that God is present. God is to humanity as a shepherd is to sheep. In the context of sheep husbandry, the shepherd is always amid the sheep, whether they are sick or healthy, whereupon the shepherd always smells like sheep. So, God carries all the provision in the universe; and from his innermost being, the universe comes into existence, worlds are continuously being created, and we were created. If this is true, then it is reasonable to accept that we carry the same divine provision. When God created man, He made him from clay of the Earth. Then, God breathed his breath into man, which caused him to come alive. The breath of God drives the being of God into our whole being; thus, everything that is inside of God, we have access to. When God breathes, He gives us life. When we breathe, we receive from God. This interconnection of breath means that the same fullness in the Father enters into us. From a Hebrew ontological perspective, man has both an upper soul and a lower soul. The lower soul is called nefesh, which God breathed into man. So, the breath of God refers to the lower soul, nefesh, because it is the same breath that gave us nefesh. Both man and animals have nephesh. When man breathes, this is not just physical function. It is a reminder to God of the fullness of God's being that is supposed to come to us. The writer of Ecclesiastes wrote, "Where there is breath, there is hope," which

אתה

refers to this interconnection of breath between God and man.

"The Lord is my shepherd; I shall not want."

Want comes from an inner sense of lack. David wrote, "I shall not want/lack/be without/go without." The word "want" is the Hebrew word "Achsar" which can translate "I shall not want" to "I shall never have an empty hand". Our hands are valuable because in our hands are written the scrolls of destiny. All the ancients believed there is a scroll written on the human hand. It is the scroll of destiny that palm readers endeavor to read. In Psalm 91:12 the bible says the angels shall bear you up in their hands. No one can undo the record of God's intent inscribed upon the palm of our hands. "I Shall" is used as an imperative, an assurance because the presence of Yahweh ensures that our hands are always full of the record and outflow of His divine intent which, according to scripture, is His good will.

If we operate from a place of lack, we can never be at rest. The answer to our restlessness could be to change our perspective toward God's capacity to provide for us.

"He leadeth me beside still waters."

The only place where still waters exist is in the throne room. In the book of Revelation, when John saw the throne of God, he saw the sea was like glass. The sea did not have any ripples in it. David knew there were still waters because he had been there, "David, the son of Jesse, the man who was taken up into heaven" (2 Samuel 23:1).

God has taken away all of our excuses for walking in lack. We claimed the devil was our problem, God conquered the devil at the cross. We said our sin was the problem, God gave his blood to wash away our sin. We said that it was darkness, God made us light. We said we have no friends, God became our friend and surrounded us with angels. When we forget the truth that Yahweh is our ever-present Provider and we will receive from Him, we remain operating in lack.

אתה

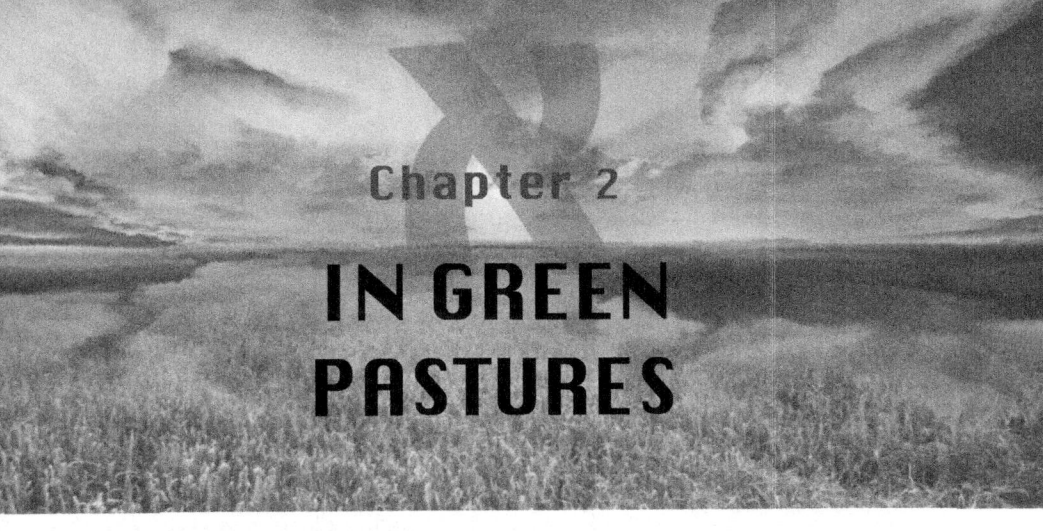

Chapter 2

IN GREEN PASTURES

> All the walls in the world are based on the idea of scarcity or anxiety; anxiety is based on an underlying sense of scarcity.

Most social systems, like politics and economics, are based on the idea of scarcity. The system of economics is based on the idea of limited resources on earth, and how those resources are controlled and appropriated so that no one person or group receives too much. Consequently, we have been trained to operate from a position of lack and scarcity, which affects everything we do. In Psalm 23, David wrote, "The Lord is my shepherd; I shall not want". This indicates how David learned to live without a sense of lack underwriting his life. It is a life without a sense of lack that David was signifying. We should be like David and operate from a place where our lives are without a sense of lack. It is not that there is no lack, rather there is no sense of lack. The Psalm says, "I shall not want". By this expression, David revealed that he placed the idea or sense of abundance in the internal structure of himself. If we would deal with the mental structure of scarcity or lack, it opens us up to the flow of abundance.

David wrote of the Lord as his shepherd. The Hebrew word for "shepherd" in Psalm 23 is "Ra'ah" (רָאָה). This is a fascinating word because it means more than a shepherd who takes care of his sheep. "Ra'ah" could translate the phrase as, 'The Lord is my way of seeing". Recall that Abraham called the Lord "Jireh" because "Jireh" (יִרְאֶה) means to see, even though it has often been said to mean provision. Therefore, Jehovah Yireh is not really the Lord is my provider; it is the Lord sees and is the way of seeing. When God created the world, first he spoke; then, he saw. This is important because our lives are

אתה

determined by both what we say and how we see. Psalm 23 may be read, "The Lord is my way of seeing; I shall not want". When we see the way God sees, it opens our being to the overflow of abundance. Every human carries within their internal structure the full record of divine provision. Until human beings see the way God sees, they are trained to see from the perspective of scarcity.

> Rest is not sleep; rest is an uncommon calmness and inner tranquility when nothing moves you within

David wrote, "He makes me lie down in green pastures."

"In the dwelling place of grassy fields, he makes me lie down or makes me rest." This verse reveals the principles and technology for harnessing and releasing the abundance within us. If a sense of scarcity causes anxiety and restlessness, then a sense of abundance causes rest. Maybe the reason for our anxiety is our focus on what we don't have, what we may never have, or our focus on others receiving it and it running out before we have our chance. This idea of scarcity is like the salesman's model: get it before it's gone! It's the last sale of the year! Every advertisement is about things are going to run out. Without rushing, without doing this or that, then it's going to run out. The next year, even with the same advertisements, we respond the same way.

In the house of the grassy meadows, He makes me to rest.

This principle of rest is always the technology for releasing the abundance or the scroll of abundance of divinity that was in God's mind and intent before he created us. Now, rest must be distinguished from sleep; rest is an uncommon calmness and inner tranquility, when nothing moves us within. Rest is being in the center of the storm where the wave doesn't exist, even though the storm is raging all around us. That is what happens if we know ourselves and we have a way of seeing that focuses on the right place. Depending on our perspective, if we look at something terrible, we may have anxiety because of what we see or we may still have peace.

God talks about rest from Genesis. The bible is replete with, "I will

אתה

give you rest"; however, rest is not a cessation from work or activity. It is an inner peace. In Africa, we say a great dancer is someone who moves and yet is still. Europeans say the dancer has grace. So, if the dancer has grace, she makes the dance look effortless. Find that center and stay there no matter what. Finding that center is not about sitting at home watching television, eating burritos and drinking coca-cola. That is not rest; it's laziness. So, resting in the depth of your being is not laziness. Too many believers think resting is stopping everything. Good warriors are always at rest in themselves.

Even God is at rest. Jesus said my Father works until now and I work also. Yet, the Bible says God rested. This is a mystery—God, who works and also is at rest, is who God is. The idea of rest is probably one of the greatest keys for unlocking the depth of what is inside of us, what is intimated in the expressions "be still and be anxious for nothing." One way to know that we have rest is if we believe something absolutely, regardless of what happens around us, because faith is an expression of rest, not mental agitation. But many have turned faith into, "You got to believe!" Truly, faith that works from rest is more powerful than faith that works from busyness. God said about Israel, "I'm not bringing them into my rest because they do not believe." So, faith creates rest, but rest gives birth to faith. If we don't believe, we will not be at peace. If we're not at peace, we won't believe.

David said, "He leads me beside still waters". The word that is used for "beside" is the word 'al (עַל) in Hebrew. This word means "upon" or "hover over" the water, not by the side of the water. It should read, "He leads me upon the waters, the still waters". Now, instead of walking by the river, we are actually in the center of the river; we are on the river. We are upon or hovering over the river. Now, David did not mean that God led him by the sea on earth because the sea on earth is not still. He was referring to the sea in heaven because it's the only place where there is a sea that produces without

> The idea of rest is probably one of the greatest keys for unlocking the depth of what is inside of you, that sense of "be still and be anxious for nothing."

OPERATING IN ABUNDANCE

agitation. In Revelation 15:2, it says, "I saw a sea and it was as quiet or as smooth as glass." It's not the sea of glass; it looks like glass because it is completely still. No matter what happens or is done to it, it has no ripple in it because it is not a sea in time; it's in the place of eternity. Nothing moves it, which means it is a sea of changelessness. If we're operating on that sea and God places us there, seasons don't matter to us because we are living at the very source of life. Time, changes, and vicissitudes do not matter. Further, water is a symbol of abundance. The sea has more creatures than the land does; it is the source of abundance. When Jacob blessed one of his sons, he alluded to the sea, "the abundance of the sea shall come to you." Being on the sea means we're standing from the place where God releases abundance upon the earth, regardless of our age, ethnicity, or physical features, etc. We are not under the sea; we are on top of the sea—a place of dominion and rulership in rest.

> Wealth is not from outside; it is from inside!

Rest is a place or state of calm that produces abundance without agitation. For example, France is one of the first nations to give workers weekends off. When France implemented this practice, many said that France was going to die economically; however, France discovered that the more they gave their people a place of rest, the more their productivity increased. As a result, France knows that when workers rest, they return to work and have more energy. Giving workers weekends off is now a law in the nation. Organizational psychologists know that workers need a break period after working three hours straight, especially manual work.

Intrinsic to natural law is the principle of rest which leads to renewal. When we operate in rest, we activate the abundance in us which restores the soul. David said, "He restores my soul". Rest is restorative process that rejuvenates us. In rejuvenation, we're producing something new every time because it gives us access to our unconscious. Conversely, until we are at rest, our unconscious is inaccessible to us. We are otherwise operating from our sub-conscious, which is where we push all of our mess. We are operating from the perspective of mess such that everything we're doing is based on our pain and our bad experiences; consequently, we cannot access the divine record of our souls that came with us from heaven. Society has trained us to operate from the perspective of mess that inclines us from rest to worry; however, when we rest, we reach into a divine consciousness that worry keeps from accessing.

We are the abundance. In terms of Capitalism, we are paid by employers for our work. But in reality, we are not paid because of the person for whom we work. We are paid because of what we carry. We take what is inside of us and we give it to someone. The person gives us cash. Wealth is not from outside; it is from the inside. The only way wealth can truly be accessed is by coming to rest. Jesus said, "Come unto me all you who labor and are heavy laden and I will give you rest." Further, the bible tells us to labor to enter into his rest. Our focus should be to come to a place of rest.

אתה

Chapter 3
PATHS OF RIGHTEOUSNESS

> Our fundamental problem is that we have been conditioned to adopt a concept of scarcity.

We were reared with the idea that things are running out. This fundamental problem prevents us from operating in the fullness of the increase of the Father. Our concept of scarcity is so embedded in our thinking that we even think God does not have enough. We cannot deny this as our way of thinking (I have talked to believers who say things like, "There are other people that God needs to take care of" and "I don't want to disturb God" or "I don't want to trouble God". I actually counsel people who say those things). This way of thinking has been ingrained in us since the time we were born; it's in our society that the people in the world are living in scarcity. We will kill each other because we think there's not enough. We get offended even over job positions because we think there's only a few positions to fill.

Two people—who quarrel over some things that they know God provides in abundance—are not thinking rationally, according to God's truth. This is indicative of the way we were conditioned to think; we operate this way. Notwithstanding, we were brought into this world with a full abundance of supply of the Father. In reality, God did not take away the supply from Adam; He only said that man is going to sweat to manifest it. The full abundance of the Father's supply is accessible, we must sweat to manifest and access it. We begin with an affirmation of the fact that we came from, operate in, live in abundance, and walk towards the manifestation of abundance because it is in us. God is not a God of lack or scarcity. God doesn't run out when it comes our turn. If we truly believe that, then our lives and the way we perceive things will be different from how we behave. David said, "The Lord is my shepherd; I shall not want." The word "want" signifies a constant perception that we need something that has not been supplied.

We worry about things that are not our responsibility. If God is the shepherd, it is the shepherd's responsibility to take the sheep to the place of supply. The sheep's responsibility is to eat when they get to the pasture. It is not the sheep's responsibility to plant grass. There is enough pasture for the sheep. Likewise, our supply is full. It is our perception that creates a block between the supply and the flow towards us. In order to make sure we have access to the supply, God makes us lie down in green pastures; He leads us beside quiet waters. He restores our souls, and He guides us in the paths of righteousness for His name's sake.

David wrote, "He leads me", or in Hebrew "He cajoles me". Cajoling does not mean forcing. Originally, the word was used to mean guiding and helping someone by gestures of kindness to get them where they're going, to encourage them to move in a certain direction. We must allow God to guide us so that we can access abundance. Guidance is not forcing. God doesn't force us to go to where the supply is. God works by showing us things, giving us insight; thus, to be able to know where the supply is, our eyes have to be opened. When Abraham was on the mountain, the Bible says, "On the mountain, the Lord is seen" (Gen. 22:14). The Hebrew text says that Abraham called the place where he was Jehovah Yireh. Previously, we discussed that Jehovah Yireh means the Lord will see to it or I will see to it, not the Lord shall provide. Abraham named the place where he was Jehovah Yireh which means on the mountain it shall be seen. This reveals that the key to provision is our capacity to see. In other words, the reality of provision is all round us. Moreover, people are making money and making wealth every day. In reality, there are principles and technologies, and things being traded daily. But if we can't see, it doesn't matter. If we can't see it, we're not going to access it. We need to learn how to truly see because it confirms, affirms, and solidifies the spiritual things into material things.

אתה

God wants us to look with the eyes of faith. Faith changes our situations to something that we can handle. It is vital how we see: if we see nothing, nothing will be there; If, when we are looking for God's supply, we say we don't see anything, then that's what we're going to get. Jesus said to Thomas those who believe without seeing are blessed (John 20:29). If we say, "Until I see it, I won't believe," then we need to see it so we can believe it. We don't need to see it in the physical, but in the spiritual. If seeing is believing to us, then we need to pray to see. If seeing is truly our problem, then we must ask God to let us see. Whether we see from in our inner being, our mind's eye, in the spirit, in our soul, then we're going to believe. And if we believe, nothing is impossible to him that believes.

> Everything in you that God put in you is meant to attract abundance.

There are many ways to see. We can learn what kind of sight we have and use that sight to discern our abundance. For example, some may not have spiritual insight, but have feeling sight because not everyone see spiritual things; however, everyone can feel something when it's around them. So, these can use their feeling as sight and train themselves to feel abundance. Because if they can feel abundance, they can probably see it. The problem we face is we feel poverty, lack, and we train ourselves to feel it. We tell ourselves stories about how everything is finished, there's no money in the house, nothing in the cupboard, no food in the house, etc. If we have trained ourselves to feel lack, scarcity, and poverty, we can train ourselves to feel abundance. Some have said that the universe bends to give to us what we feel because we attract it to ourselves.

Everything in us that God put in us is meant to attract abundance. Even though we may misuse it, the origin of it is not evil. If it is used appropriately and rightly, it will attract what we need in life. Our feeling is magnetic. Some of the older generation would spend time developing, what they called, their "magnetic personality". With this practice, they were feeling what they desire. We can do the same by taking passages of Scripture that deal with abundance and speaking it over ourselves so that our physical bodies can feel it. When we feel

אתה

something, it affects everything. To feel it, we must put our voice to it. We have so much available to us. We are not like the ancients who had to speak into walls and have it echo back to them. This is one reason why the ancient cathedrals were built that when they spoke, the sound echoes back to them and their bodies vibrate a certain frequency that allowed them to access something. The echo in cathedrals is not just noise. They produced a vibrational frequency that when it echoes from the walls or ceiling, it bounces back to your body. These things are available to us; with our best, joyful, and faithful voice, we can take all those passages of abundance, increase, and overflow, record them, and play it back while we sleep. We can use our own voice, not the voice of others. Nevertheless, we must pray to see. Many places in scripture in which someone prayed for something, God opened his eyes, and he saw—Haggai, Saul, Jacob, and Abraham, for example. Abraham looked behind him and saw the lamb. He looked, saw, and took it. Notwithstanding, we're still missing something. The Jews were poor people for many generations—the poorest people on earth. The jews were extremely impoverished because God spent 40 years showing them the wealth of heaven, something that a Jew can see the cause of. We can do the same thing. God brought us from heaven so we have the capacity to see the things of heaven. We have the capacity to see the fullness of what is there.

> God calls you to open your eyes.

Psalm 23:3, David said, "He guides me in the paths of righteousness." Many times, it has been quoted as "He leads me in the path of righteousness"; however, it is not a single path. The way is one, but the paths are many. Jesus listed some of these paths in the ten Beatitudes. These paths are also found in all of Jesus' commandments in Matthew chapters 5, 6, and 7. Jesus taught about thirty-two ways for us to behave. He did not teach these things as something to just do. He gave us a way of accessing fullness. We separate the beatitudes from the rest of the commandments in Matthew because we are overly influenced by chapter and verse. Jesus' teaching was a whole teaching that wasn't separated with verses. When we take it as a whole, it's really about living out the fullness of God and the fullness of heaven. For example, "Blessed are the poor in spirit for they shall inherit the earth." In fact, all the parables are about business and accessing overflow and abundance.

In many of the parables, the pattern is that a man sees something, he finds it, and then he sees it. God calls us to open our eyes. He wants to lead us by showing us how to open our eyes. In Nigeria, the people have a saying: Shine your eye. This means to wake up and see what is really going on. Our eyes are important. We must shine our physical eyes, spiritual eyes, eyes of our souls, the eyes of our bodies, and listen carefully to how the Lord is leading us in all those dimensions.

In scripture, righteousness is tied to prosperity. God leads us in paths of righteousness. And our definition of righteous is not God's definition of righteous. The truth is we already know that we are not righteous; however, walking on Paths of righteousness does not mean that we do everything right. In Isaiah 35:8, God said that He will build a highway whereupon not even a cripple or fool will err or go astray from it. If walking on the Paths of righteousness was dependent on us doing everything right, then we're going to wait forever. We must not continue to think this way because paths of righteousness is actually a path of attachment and love for God, there are many.

Proverbs 8:1-3 says,

Does not wisdom call, and understanding [a]lift up her voice?
² On top of the heights beside the way, Where the paths meet, she takes her stand;
³ Beside the gates, at the opening to the city,
At the entrance of the doors, she cries out (NASB)

When we start reading through the text, we read that Solomon said that if you listen to his voice, you're going to have riches and wealth. Wealth is the crown of a wise man. When God gave him the commandments for Israel, Moses said, "For this is your wisdom." Wisdom is a person—both a woman and a man. According to scripture, Wisdom said that she's a woman; it is referred to as "she". Wisdom is your first consult; it knew you before your DNA was put on earth. Also, the Bible says, "Jesus Christ, the wisdom of God" (1 Cor. 1:30). Thus, wisdom is both son and mother. Wisdom is the reason that

אתה

Jesus, when he was on the cross, said to John, "Behold your mother! Woman, behold your son!" Wisdom speaks this way, according to the ancients, because she is always pregnant with abundance. Wisdom is not the practical idea of ordering things to come to pass. In the book of Proverbs, wisdom is not building anything. Wisdom prays in the presence of God; it plays and dances in the presence of God.

True wisdom is enjoying what God does; however, we can't enjoy what God does, if we're concerned about what God hasn't done. Wisdom is not the thing we insist that it is, especially when we put practical in front of it. Proverbs 8:22-31 again reads,

"The LORD possessed me at the beginning of His way, Before His works of old.

From everlasting I was established,

From the beginning, from the earliest times of the earth. "When there were no depths I was brought forth, When there were no springs abounding with water. "Before the mountains were settled,

Before the hills I was brought forth;

While He had not yet made the earth and the fields, Nor the first dust of the world.

"When He established the heavens, I was there, When He inscribed a circle on the face of the deep, When He made firm the skies above,

When the springs of the deep became fixed, When He set for the sea its boundary

So that the water would not transgress His command, When He marked out the foundations of the earth; Then I was beside Him, as a master workman;

And I was daily His delight, Rejoicing always before Him, Rejoicing in the world, His earth,

And having my delight in the sons of men.

Wisdom rejoiced when there was nothing there, and She rejoiced and danced whenever He created something. She was there when He put a circle on nothingness, and She watched and rejoiced with Him.

אתה

She rejoiced with the sons of men before they were on the earth. Real wisdom enjoys what God has done or what God is doing; Wisdom does not complain about what God is not doing.

> Ask God to give you sight to see where your abundance is located. You might be shocked to realize that God points back to you.

One of the paths of righteousness is a path of interconnection between God and us. This path leads to complete abundance as we enjoy and rejoice in what God does. The reason for our continuous lack, poverty, and limitations is we don't value what's been given to us. We're constantly looking for something, and we don't realize that the joy we bring to what is present is what causes the open door to increase. For example, if someone gives children a penny or a dollar, they are very happy. But if someone gives their friend a dollar, they forget that they have a dollar and start fighting for their friend's dollar. When we think our is not enough, we can tend to behave as children. The idea that we are the key to our own breakthrough, prosperity, and abundance is solidly biblical.

We must ask God to give us sight to see where our abundance is located; God will point back to you. We must learn how to see what is inside of us. We must get wisdom—not learning how to craft something but doing what wisdom did in the presence of love—by rejoicing in what we have and speaking well of what we have. If we do this, then what we have will release its fragrance to us. We don't need the whole world; we just need a seed to sing over, rejoice over, even in the midst of chaos.

In this season, God spoke to me, "I want to expose my people to a heart of abundance." He did not tell me He is going to give us money; He told me, "I will expose them to a heart of abundance." There is sufficiency in the world; the world will not run out. There is enough for everyone. God didn't create us and decide that when we were born the abundance will stop. Regardless of any circumstance, we carry the same abundance. Our current situations and struggles are meant to shock us into the next level of our abundance. We must focus our mind on the abundance. We must let our feelings receive the abundance. We must celebrate what is in our hands. We cannot be lazy. A lazy person can't praise and worship God for what is present because it takes all his strength and power to do so. It takes strength not to complain when everything in us is saying complain or to rejoice in the midst of what seems like nothing is going right. The person who is worshiping and celebrating God in what he has is actually a strong person.

Chapter 4
WALKING IN THE SHADOW

Even though I walk through the valley of the shadow of death.
I fear no evil. For you are with me;
Your rod and Your staff. They comfort me. (NASB)

...How do we as believers still operate under this principle of abundance in the context of the shadow of death?

When David wrote, "I walk through the valley of the shadow of death," he quoted Job. Job used the phrase "shadow of death" negatively, at least five times to mean "the shadow of my life is disappearing". From Job's perspective, a shadow is fleeting, temporary, and shifting; it is not constant. It is dark and evasive (In my native tradition, we talk about the tree of life and we talk about the shadow trees). Shadows or "shade", in the English tradition, are like demons. There is a shadow that keeps us from or even kills the flow of divine wealth, divine prosperity, divine overflow and abundance in our lives. When we are in position in line for the flow of the prosperity, the fundamental nature of the shepherd, the flow of the shepherd's heart and all that comes with it, to receive that which comes out of rest, shifting events, like shadows, come into our lives. They are meant to create attitudes, ideas, or responses that hinder our capacity to receive what is flowing from our shepherd into our lives. When David wrote, "Even though I walk through the valley of the shadow of death, I will fear no evil," he meant that it's not really necessary for us to be in the shadow of death because God has already told us our position.

אתה

Read these verses again:

> The Lord is my shepherd, I shall not want.
> He makes me lie down in green pastures; He leads me
> beside quiet waters.
> He restores my soul;
> He guides me in the paths of righteousness
> For His name's sake.
> He's already told us our position. We don't have to stay
> in the valley of the shadow of death.

In Ephesians 1:3, it says,

> Blessed be the God and Father of our Lord Jesus Christ, who has blessed us with every spiritual blessing in the heavenly places in Christ (NASB)

This world is not a world of shadow. Shadows move according to the position of light. If there is a shadow, you have to ask which kind of shadow is it and where the light is positioned to cast the shadow.

There is a shadow of death and a shadow of life. There is the shadow of the wing of God. The type of shadow depends on which type of light it is coming from. The shadow of death is the result of a false light that is thrown upon our lives to draw our eyes and minds away from where we are seated, as revealed in the first three verses of Psalm 23. When we are in the valley of the shadow of death, we have to realize that the shadow is cast by a false kind of light.

> If you begin to depend on something other than that which is established in the spiritual realm, you create a false shadow upon yourself.

God has all that we need. He is not holding anything back from us. He wants to work in our lives. He wants us to prosper. Even though we know this is true, when certain circumstances arise, we begin to believe transient issues and conditions, things that people say to us, and things we say to ourselves.

4 : Walking in the shadow

אַתָּה

Then, we begin to depend on predictions of the economy and all negative things that could happen in the world. If we begin to depend on something other than that which is established in the spiritual realm, we create a false shadow upon ourselves, which kills. It first kills our concentration and puts our focus on what we already know by creating doubt. And doubt is a shadow of death. Conversely, faith is a shadow of light. Faith proclaims, "even though I walk through the valley of the shadow of death, I will not fear evil."

One way to overcome false shadows and to change shadows is to keep moving. We should never allow ourselves to be stuck in what happens to us because it will kill and destroy us. Continuing to walk and keep moving is a way to deal with the shadow of death.

Doubt and fear go hand-in-hand. Both will keep us stuck in the valley of the shadow of death. When David said, "Though I walk through the valley of the shadow of death," he listed what the shadows are: Doubt is a shadow; fear is a shadow; a lack of vision, which is blindness, is a shadow. When we lack vision, we are blind, and we are in the shadow of death. "Where there is no vision, the people perish," (Provbers 29:18, KJV).

> Being stuck in the valley of the shadow of death produces the shadow of blame.

Lack of vision will throw us into a spiraling abyss. When we are stuck in the valley of the shadow of Death in which we are doubting, fearful, and lacking vision, our tendency should be to find out who or what is it that is stopping us from being able to move. As long as we are stuck in the valley of the shadow of Death, we are not permitted to see who we are, positively or negatively. When someone talks about himself negatively, he is looking for someone to blame. Someone asks, "Why do I do this or why am I in this situation?". He will first blame the devil, who gets all the blame. He may even blame God. He will likely never blame himself. Being stuck in the valley of the shadow of death produces the shadow of blame.

When we walk through the valley of the shadow of death, we don't have to fear evil "for You are with me; Your rod and Your staff, they comfort me" (Psalm 23:4). In the Hebrew, "You" is Atta (אַתָּה), a

אתה

reference to God's name.

You [are]   >   'at·tāh   >   אַתָּה

In Old English, Atta is translated as Thou, which is a reference for royalty. When we say "You" today, it is a common reference that could be used for anyone. However, in this instance, the "You" carries this meaning of royalty and respect.

David said that the reason we can deal with the shadows is Atta is with us—Aleph, Tav, Heh (אתה). If we remove the Heh, we are left with Aleph Tav, which is Alpha and Omega. The Alpha is the first letter in Atta; it opens an otherwise closed system. In other words, we don't have to be afraid in the valley of the shadow of death because we are in a system that's always open for possibility. Because Atta is with us, possibility is with us. .   There is another shadow called [foreign 1:20:15] or in the Hebrew [foreign 1:20:18].   The bible says in Psalm 91,

> He who dwells in the secret place of the Most High
> Shall abide under the shadow of the Almighty. (NKJV)

Let's look again at the Hebrew for "I will fear no evil" which is pronounced "Lo yi ra ra."

rā'	'î·rā	lō-
רָא	יְרָא	לֹא
evil	I will fear	no

"Yi ra" is a combination of the Yod Resh and Aleph. The word for evil is Resh Aleph. "Yod" is added to Resh Aleph (evil); it indicates that this is the hand of God and standing over evil. "Ra" is evil but "yira" is to stand above evil. In the valley of the shadow of death, we fear no evil because Atta is with us. We walk with open possibilities before us; we can keep moving forward. We will never get stuck in the shadow of death because we understand who is with us. Atta is with me and His rod and staff comfort me.

אתה

The Rod and Staff are really two pillars in the House of God that He uses to comfort us—mercy and strength. His mercy and strength are the reasons for our comfort.

yenachamuni	**heimmah**
יְנַחֲמֻנִי	הֵמָּה
comfort me	they

We can remember Atta is with us, opening possibilities, and mercy is on our right hand and strength is on the left hand. Strength and mercy are not providing future comfort, as if just to comfort us in the future; they create a position of rest for us now, presently. Our goal is to put ourselves in a position of rest to receive what the Father has already spoken in the beginning of Psalm 23. When we are in the context of the shadow of death, we must find rest because these shadows come to shift us away from rest whereby making it impossible for us to receive what truly belongs to us. Because of agitation, we miss our moment.

In our world, greedy and powerful men are trying to create a system of fear; we have to stay in a position of rest. Regardless of any of our various persuasions, we are walking in the valley of the shadow of death. Many things are emerging in the world but a believer cannot allow these circumstances to keep them from understanding that Atta is always present; mercy and strength are always present to provide comfort and rest. We must learn to stay in this position of rest it allows the believer to receive in the midst of agitation, to prosper in the midst of the valley of the shadow of death, and to bring forth life even where there is death.

While these shadows are cast to remove our focus from rest, they are not permanent. The shadows are temporary, especially the shadow of death. Only the shadow under the wing of God is permanent. It is the shadow of El Shaddai—the name of provision. If we are under the shadow of El Shaddai, we are really living under perfect light. The Father's shadow is a shadow of light, not darkness, doubt, or destruction.

It says in Psalm 121:5:

> The Lord is your keeper;
> The Lord is your shade on your right hand.

In this text, David was not referring to the same shadow in Psalm 23 because God is light; there is no darkness in His shadow. Imagine light hitting someone and his shadow becomes like bright light, instead of blocking light. David was revealing this about the shadow of the Father. So, in the shadow of the wing of God, God transfers His light into our circumstances. It is a second shadow, perhaps, that flows into our context when we are in the valley of the shadow of death. In other words, we always have a shadow of light present. It seems contradictory—a shadow is light. It is light that is a clear, translucent manifestation of divinity in the context of our darkness.

> I will not fear any evil for thou art with me;
> thy rod and thy staff they comfort me.
> Comfort and rest are the basis of miracles.

> "Comfort, yes, comfort My people!" Says your God. "Speak comfort to Jerusalem, and cry out to her That her warfare is ended,

> That her iniquity is pardoned..." (Isaiah 40:1-2a, NKJV)

In this context of scripture, when God spoke about comfort, He said that no matter what someone is going through, the trials are already past; the pain that came before is already healed. God said to tell her, Jerusalem, that her warfare is over. When God speaks comfort to us in our context of suffering, it means that our suffering is already done.

When a word of comfort comes to us, we should accept that we are already delivered from the situation in which we find ourselves; otherwise, God would not speak comfort to us. Comfort is a harbinger of Good news.

אתה

Isaiah 40:9 says:

> O Zion,
> You who bring good tidings, Get up into the high mountain; O Jerusalem,
> You who bring good tidings, Lift up your voice with strength, Lift it up, be not afraid;
> Say to the cities of Judah, "Behold your God!"
> (NKJV)

When the word of comfort comes and when Jesus said, "They shall be comforted," it means that there's always a flow of good news and a flow of open possibilities in the context of what we're going through. It is not that we will not find ourselves in a shadow of darkness; however, if we find ourselves in a shadow of darkness we don't really have to be in it. Many shadows we walk in, we walk into ourselves. If we are in the context of the valley of the shadow of death, we must understand that because Atta is with us, there's mercy, strength, and comfort. Comfort means that there is good news in the context of the suffering—God has already made the decision that our future is present in the context of that shadow. God does not leave us in the shadow. He comforts us to bring us out of the valley of the shadow of death and into the shadow of His wing, the valley of the shadow of the Almighty. He's telling us to stand up, move, and go home.

> I'm learning that God doesn't wait for the situation to be over to comfort you.

God doesn't wait for the situation to be over to comfort us. This is evident in the way God dealt with Job; He visited Job while Job was suffering. When God visited Job, Job still continued to suffer. In reality, God was already there looking at Job; He was already there comforting Job through Elihu (Job 32-38). God, Atta, was present in the context of Job's suffering.

"Atta" (אַתָּה) is Aleph Tav Heh, in Hebrew. Aleph is the principle of creation that God put for Himself in order to have an ace to remove the world from every condition into which it enters. For Atta, it means that, not only is the Aleph of the precreation principle present, but the Aleph of the future world is present as well.

Regardless of what we may be going through, there is no valley of the shadow where Atta is not present. There is always open possibility in our circumstances because we are the open possibility. We can never be enclosed so much that we can't come out. We are sons and daughters of God and Atta is with us. If we cannot catch the wind, or hold heaven and bind it with the string, or take God and make Him our prisoner, then it is impossible for us to be held captive such that we cannot get out. Our suffering may endure a while but our God will not fail us. It is not the end of our life; it can never be. There is always an opening and there is always a comfort for us. God's comfort means that our future has already come to our present. Amen.

Chapter 5
GOD'S TABLE

> Supernatural provision and the overwhelming flow of God's providence towards those who are his children is not a prosperity-gospel message; however, it is a message that includes the idea of having wealth.

The struggle appropriating wealth is connected to the measure and degree to which we are operating from a place of lack in everything. Operating from lack is what triggers comparison with others. Operating from lack is what makes us think that something is being taken away from us. When we operate from the perspective that something is being taken away from us, we cease and are unable to actually harvest the fullness of what is in the present. We must learn to believe that being blessed means living in the fullness of who God is. It is not that God is blessed because we give him blessing; God is blessed because it is His intrinsic personality.

When we bless God and speak well of Him, we activate that fullness of God and it is released to flow through us. We add nothing to God; we take nothing from God. We must become so full and understand the fullness of ourselves, we don't feel like something is being taken away from us when someone comes into our presence. This is a very important Christian principle, but it is hard for people to learn; we are taught, our whole lives, that people who come into our lives are trying to take something away from us. However, no matter how it is couched, whether in religious or spiritual terms, it is not Christian to respond this way because nothing is being taken away from us. It is imperative for us to change this way of thinking because it leads to serious problems in society and in our personal lives. When we operate from this faulty perspective, it means we don't believe in the ever-flowing fullness of God to which we are connected. We have been trained, as a society, to believe that the universe is based on fundamental lack, not on fundamental plenitude. So, we bite, beat, hurt, and fight each other because we think something is being taken away from us. Truly, God, who created the universe, doesn't suffer lack; consequently, the universe is based on fundamental plenitude, fundamental purification, and a fundamental capacity to reproduce, to restore, to rectify, to reunify, and to heal itself. This is a completely different perspective than what we have been trained to have.

> We must understand that the God who created the universe doesn't suffer lack.

Our perspective of lack informs how we approach many areas of our lives. For example, if we approach relationships from the perspective of lack, there can never be any real trust because we are always expecting that the other person just wants to take something from us. And we will end up trying to benefit or "be on top" in the relationship by drawing from the other person's fullness despite their weakness. Operating in lack leads to corruption of our own motives and intent as well.

When David declared, "Thou prepares a table before me," he was revealing what God is providing for us, the protocol of God's table, and how we must prepare ourselves to come to the table. In 1563, Joseph Karo, one of the great rabbis, wrote Shulcan Aruch, which means "the preparation of the table". In his five-volume work concerning the law, Karo wrote about how one prepares himself to keep the law, and how to prepare oneself to preach. The practice of preparation is one thing that makes Jews different. Jews will spend much time preparing themselves for worship. It seems like just an ostentatious practice, which some will doubtless call religious; notwithstanding, what seems to be discarded or regarded as religious, Jews call it preparation. We must be careful how we misuse the word religious. Every time someone prepares himself to do something for God, or practices a spiritual activity, or prepare for coming before God, many Christians call it "religious". Many Christians, if they are invited to pray five times a day,

אתה

won't do it because they see it as superficial, meaningless, "religious" activity. Ironically, if they invited a king to a table, they would make preparation with alacrity but would not call the preparation "religious". This is our thinking and what we have done to ourselves: by calling or dismissing everything as "religious", we are freeing ourselves from actually engaging God in His fullness. And these are the very things that actually activate the fullness of God in our lives. Perhaps all our language about things being religious is from the devil and not from God because it stops believers from doing what they're supposed to do to access the fullness of who they are. We become our own worst enemies by condemning the very things that empower our own spirituality growth, which we call spirituality.

> When we operate from lack and the perspective that an enemy must always be an enemy, we want to eat alone and make sure our enemies have nothing to eat.

The word ta'aroch shulcan means "You prepare a table". This table is prepared facing us in our presence; however, there is no place in scripture that says that table is prepared for us. Many interpret Psalm 23:5 as God has prepared a table for us in front of our enemies so they can watch us eating. Rather, the table is prepared before us in the presence of our enemies so that they may participate with us and be transformed. This could signify that God's table is a divine transmutation or principle whereby all are invited to participate and be transformed. Jesus taught his disciples about changing perspective about their enemies. He told them to love their enemies and pray for them when they curse them (Matthew 5:44). In Romans 12:20, Paul, quoting Proverbs, wrote to feed our enemy if he is hungry. When we have a fundamental sense of lack it skews our perspective—our enemy must always be our enemy. When we operate from lack with that perspective, we want to eat alone and make sure our enemies have nothing to eat. We want to make sure that those who are more wicked than us cannot participate at God's table. This perspective doesn't make us righteous. Ta'aroch shulcan, is an important idea: preparing ourselves and the practice of preparation is transmutational because it speaks of God's deliberate intention. When God prepares this table, He intentionally does so. He does not haphazardly throw food on the table in front of someone. This same God who prepares the table before us is the same God who provides for the world, even for our enemies.

If God prepares His table out of the fullness of His being, He must be preparing it so that all who are around us can benefit from it.

Perhaps we have a perspective in life that is so colored by society and our ideology, we usually don't have the capacity to step outside and look at these types of things objectively. We think our enemies must always suffer. The truth is our enemies are invited to sit at the table and be transformed. This is the grace of God because while we were yet enemies of God, we were reconciled to Him through Christ's death (Romans 5:10). If the interpretation of Psalm 23:5 is God prepares food so we can eat and our enemies can suffer, this is unlike what God did for us when he invited us to participate at His table while we were still His enemies. God prepared a table in front of Israel so that we, even as an enemy, can partake and become whole. But here our ideology goes awry. Whilst we preach the fullness of the Holy Spirit and the fullness of sanctification, we don't have this in our ideology that the fullness must overflow to our enemies.

> God does not bless me so that my enemies can eat their heart out.

This means that when we are eating in the presence of God, our enemies are in the presence of God with us. We bring them with us. Eating with God must include our enemies because it is through our fellowship with God that our enemies become transmuted. If we leave them out, there is nowhere they can experience transformation. We cannot change the world if we refuse our enemies and eat alone. This is some of the challenge and difficulty in Christianity, church growth, and having fellowship: our enemies must participate despite themselves. We must include them. Perhaps we want to have a type of Christianity in which our enemies are far away; however, our duty is to create a world in which there are no enemies. We do that by bringing our

אתה

enemies to participate in the fellowship, not by keeping our enemies afar. Love is a transmutational key. Jesus said love can change anyone. In fact, the preparation of the table in the presence of my enemy is a transmutational key that exemplifies God's intrinsic nature and how we can be like Him.

> Everything He is doing for you, He's doing for the salvation of the world to turn all of us around.

We must invite our enemies to participate at the table, even our internal enemies. While our ideology has us keeping our enemies far away, we are still eating in the presence of our enemies—our internal enemies. Our internal enemies are with us while we eat. We don't wait until they are removed before we eat. God teaches us a lot about how He deals with us when David said, "Thou preparest a table before me". The word translated as "before me" is the Hebrew word "lefenay" (לְפָנַי); this word literally means "in front of me" or "in my face". Whilst it is usually translated as "before me", it should be translated "towards my face". Consequently, the actual participation in the table is a face-to-face encounter with the enemy. Is it possible to transform an enemy if we are unwilling to talk with them face-to-face? Until we encounter them face-to-face, we can't change them.

We must remember that God's table is not a personal or private table; it is a public table because our enemies are around it as well. God's table is transformational and transmutational. God prepares it. It is His table, not ours. Through the transmutational nature of his love, He gives us the permission to participate.

God prepares His table right in front of us, in our faces, so that we can participate in His banquet. When our enemies witness this, they themselves will also be transformed.

God does not bless us so that our enemies can eat their hearts out. He blesses us so our enemies can see how good He is and turn in repentance to Him. God operates from the position of fullness, not lack. Everything he is doing for us, He does for the salvation of the world to turn all of us around.

אתה

Chapter 6

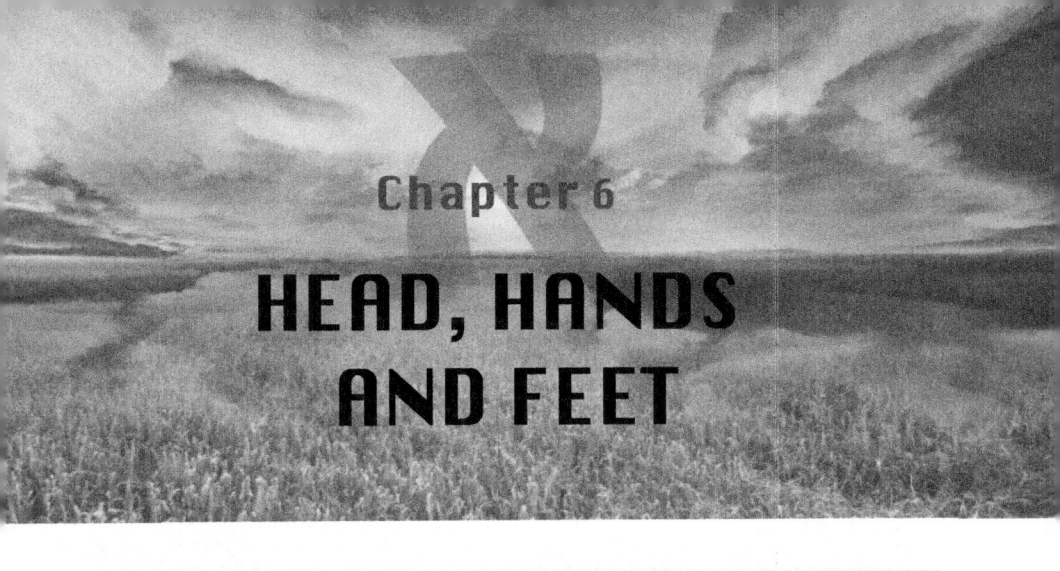

HEAD, HANDS AND FEET

> By the end of this chapter, we will see that Psalm 23 is really about an overflowing, super abundant life.

We will consider the two together. We—spirit-filled believers with all our prophetic, evangelistic and charismatic perspectives—have many things to say about anointing. Here, the word used for "anoint" is the Hebrew word deshanta; it means to make fat, to cause to expand, to cause to completely purify. It has the same root as Mashiach, which is the anointed one or messiah. However, the structure of deshanta is different that Mashiach. It seems that David used this word very deliberately.

When someone is called the anointed one, it means he has been given a load or something has been put upon him that allows him to bear whatever is coming his way. In other words, the anointed one is given a seed that brings forth a purpose; however, When David said, "Thou anointest my head with oil", it is the head that is being anointed because He literally rubs oil upon the head. In the Likkutei Amarim, a book of Jewish mysticism, it says there is a soul in the human brain and that this soul contains the Chabad, which is wisdom, understanding, and knowledge. When David unfolded this revelation about walking in abundance, he said that the head or rosh (ראש) is important for the opening of abundance. How our heads work determines whether we prosper or whether we don't. If you give a fool wealth, he or she will squander it (Proverbs 21:20). Solomon complained about this; he was doing all the work to prosper his kingdom and wasn't sure if the one to whom he was leaving it was going to be a foolish or wise person.

אתה

> The idea of anointing is a powerful thing. Anointing readies the person or object for the reception of the glory and the intention of God in Whose presence a person stands or in Whose presence an object is used.

Deshanta means to fatten and grown; this is why David focused on anointing the head. Further, it is the anointing of kings that is always done on the head. In addition to kings and priests, God instructs the Jews to anoint ordinary things and smear them with oil like sticks, the tabernacle, altars, Aaron's garments, even the utensils of the tabernacle. Sometimes the word can also be used for the removal of ashes that have been burnt upon an altar.

What David has focused on with respect to anointing is powerful. The anointing readies a person or object for the reception of the glory and intention of God. It is in God's presence a person stands and in whose presence an object is used. Without the anointing, it cannot receive the glory and purpose of the One in whose presence it is supposed to be manifest. So, the anointing is given, first of all, to make the person a place, or to make the person usable or ready for the entrance of the glory because the anointing without the glory is nothing but oil, making something oily.

The anointing is always for God's purpose. David said that the anointing, as referenced in this text of scripture, is only on the head because the intellectual process is important to God for making a person prosperous. It is more than just praying and asking to do a miracle. The way we use our heads determines whether we prosper or not.

The Pentecostal church, by and large, has not taught people how to use their heads to make wealth. We have taught them how to use their knees to make wealth, as in prayer. But using the head is important. The head contains three things: the left brain, the right brain, and the soul, which is wisdom, understanding, and knowledge. If the head is what receives the anointing, then the brain serves as a funnel for the entrance of things from the supernatural realm into this realm. We deceive ourselves if we think we're actually going to

אתה

transform people if we don't expect people to think in church and we talk to them at the lowest common level. This is unfruitful, inexpedient, and a waste of time. Even when people complain that something is being communicated above their understanding, we must urge them to come up higher. We must not continue to speak to others as if they are dumb, foolish, or ignorant, when what is in them is greater than what they can ever be taught. When David emphasized the importance of anointing the head, he called attention to the need to engage our intellects in this process of operating in abundance.

We can't actually even be a holy person without using our intellects because holiness is making choices to do good things based on God's direction. The Jewish practice is mitzvah, which is an intentional obedience to the law and choosing to perform acts of kindness. Holiness must be both experiential and cerebral—our brains must be involved. When we come to church, we must also engage our brains—our thinking. This does not make our spiritual fellowship about arguments and debates because that kind of dynamic is counterproductive. We must allow our brains to function also. In the intent of our hearts, the soul and brain work together, and it is made functional through our hands. In other words, the intent of our hearts never comes to pass until we engage our souls. God anoints our heads because it is the magnetic point at which the supernatural realm enters our beings.

> Revelation is a combination of wisdom, understanding, and knowledge.

In church, we talk very much about the heart, whereas we don't talk much about the head; consequently, we have become very sentimental in church. Some Christians may get offended when you attempt to engage them intellectually. Then, it may be difficult to challenge them. When these kinds of Christians enter the world where there are structures, patterns, and paradigms for performance, they don't want to engage. They often want a shortcut; they don't want to engage areas about which they have never previously thought. They find it difficult to have to think about it and figure it out. Further, our lack of inclusion of insights about the head in our churches has

אתה

perhaps created our reliance on miracles. Now, this does not mean that a rationalistic process solves anything. The reason for the anointing is to combine our intellectual process with our God-given wisdom, understanding, and knowledge.

The information-gathering process of collecting and then analyzing data must be combined with divine revelation. The equation is: information-gathering plus divine revelation; we cannot eliminate one piece of this equation. Some people only have data or hearsay, nothing more. Only having data or hearsay without revelation is ineffective. Some people believe they have revelation but it is not combined with knowledge. If God gives someone revelation, He will give the necessary information to support it.

> Anointing is a way to expand you to be able to handle what you have been given to do.

Revelation is a combination of wisdom, understanding, and knowledge. Knowledge is the result of combining facts, information, and data. For example, a baby is born by knowledge. The bible says Adam knew his wife (Genesis 4:1). The procreative process involved two people: father and mother. It also includes wisdom and understanding to produce this knowledge. A baby is the manifestation of the knowledge of father and mother. Some of the great rabbis assert that it is the father's brain that conceives the baby before the semen gets into the mother' womb, then he plants the seed. A baby is not just a result of a physical act; the baby is the manifestation of a cognitive process that is activated in the man's brain. It then is released and goes into the woman to gestate for nine months. After nine months, it is delivered as knowledge—a baby. Thus, children are the consummation of knowledge, wisdom, and understanding that started from another realm and came as anointing upon the head. How powerful it is to look at our children from this perspective.

Deshanta is the Hebrew word translated "anoint". Deshanta can also mean to remove the burnt ashes on the altar. When God anoints our heads, when the anointing comes upon us, it is also for the purpose of decluttering our minds. When the anointing comes upon someone, it

אתה

declutters the mind. There is no anointing where the mind is cluttered. A part of the process of anointing is for our minds and our brains to be decluttered and for the ashes of generations of bad thinking to be cleansed. Consider David, he was from a line of incest. According to scripture, David was a great man, but his father's relationship with his mother was problematic; however, the anointing removed that and opened new vistas of understanding about who David was, his relationship with the world, and what he was supposed to accomplish. Consider Jesus Christ, he is a man born from a woman who said she saw an angel. Throughout Jesus' life, the Jews demanded, "Show us your father. Is this not the son of Mary or Joseph the carpenter?" The Jews often had words for him. Even though Jesus was God as a man, it may have been difficult to walk around town and hear people wonder about him in the way they did, especially because Jesus knew what they were thinking in their hearts. Imagine Jesus walking around his city his entire life hearing people say, "Yeah, right! His mother saw an angel. It must be one of the Roman soldiers that was the angel." Nevertheless, because of the anointing, the chatter never took ascendency in his life. Jesus never talked about it. He focused his mind so that it was clear from the clutter of human conversation about his identity. Some people, with that kind of background, always mix their mess with the message. It's avsy about them because of their father's failure, but this is not so with Jesus Christ.

> So the anointing is the expansion of your consciousness and your capacity to receive from the fullness of who God is in your life.

Jesus was not anointed at birth. He was anointed at his baptism. Being a son of God is not the same as being anointed. The anointing is only needed for certain work or for a thought process that will produce God's desired result. The anointing on the head means that His consciousness is being expanded to be able to handle the greatness of the desire and the thought of God for his life. Further, the anointing is the expansion of our consciousness and our capacity to receive from the fullness of who God is in our lives. Therefore, if God says he wants to use us to change the world, we could not handle it ordinarily, unless God brings something that expands our capacity to

OPERATING IN ABUNDANCE

47

אתה

handle it.

God anoints us to expand us to be able to handle our God-given assignment. After we have completed our respective assignments or tasks for which God has anointed us, we can't perform it anymore because the anointing was released for the momentary assignment. We can't perform it anymore because the anointing was released to create an expansiveness and capacity to handle the greater and momentary responsibility from God. To that end, we should never boast about being anointed because the anointing does not belong to us; it is released for the God-given work. For example, if someone receives an anointing for speaking, everyone may think how powerful he is, until it goes to his head. He may think that it is all his ability; nevertheless, when the anointing lifts, people see his human frailties. The anointing has a beautifying effect which allows people to listen to things he is saying, otherwise, they may not listen to him if the anointing is not there. In scripture, Aaron was an idol worshipper, who at a certain time called Satan from Hell; however, Aaron was changed by the anointing. When the anointing had come on him, he had become the high priest and was able to open up Heaven. The anointing is effective; even sticks made into utensils became carriers of divine presence, after being rubbed with oil.

The genuine anointing from God does not stay on the head; it flows on to the hand. David said, "My cup runneth over"; that is, prosperity comes by the head and the hand. A cup bearer, when serving the table, doesn't sit the cup on the table to let it automatically run over. He tips or bends the cup over to release what is in it. The Hebrew word for "cup" is "kavas"(כוס); it beings with the letter Kaph. Kaph can mean something that is so overwhelmingly grievous that the burden is too much to bear; however, Kaph can also mean something that is bent to release what is in it. Kaph, like the hand, can carry but also pour out.

> Angels will help you when you stretch your hand out, but you're sitting around waiting for things to manifest.

David showed the significance of the running-over cup: it connects

אתה

the hand and the head (I am writing to this generation—those who say they are anointed but don't want to do the work and use their hands. Instead, they sit passively, fast for 25 days, and wait for God to download a miracle). The anointing must flow through the cup of the hand because wealth comes from head to hand. If God wants to prosper us, He will give us an idea of what to do. He will put something in our heads that we can work out through our hands. After the anointing came upon his hand, David said, "Blessed is the Lord that teaches my hand to work."

> God gives you the power to make wealth

It is not biblical that we don't have to use our hands because God will just drop things from heaven. Even though there are times when God does miracles, we don't lounge about waiting for angels to clean our houses. God promised us wealth; however, He promised to put ideas in our heads and to strengthen our hands to bring it to pass. He put the record in the palm of our hands. Moses prayed in Psalm 90:17, "And establish the work of our hands for us; Yes, establish the work of our hands" (NKJV). When we receive ideas in our heads, we must work it out. Angels will help us when we stretch out our hands. The angels cannot see the record of our scrolls if we don't stretch out our hands. We can't be passive just waiting for the ideas in our heads to manifest.

Many times, many people have told me that they want to teach and travel around the world like me. I tell them straightforwardly that they are too lazy and only want to have fun because what I do requires much work. I advise them how I spend my time. I advise them that it is not unusual for me to return from vacation at 3AM, go to my office to prepare for what I'm teaching the next morning. We cannot rely on our personal brilliance or capacity to recount information; we must be able to receive from heaven, having our wisdom in our brains, and understanding and knowledge working together as a triangular downward funnel to bring the supernatural realm into this realm. In this way, it reaches out influencing how we do things with our hands, ten fingers, ten principles of creation, ten commandments. Life is not a lottery.

אתה

Our Father is always speaking. There is no special time when God is downloading. Every time we pray, God is speaking and downloading. God anoints our heads to expand our consciousness to receive what He is speaking and downloading. Because God is giving us ideas, we must use our heads and think. We must develop a consistent practice of being still to listen to receive ideas from heaven. The ideas that God releases to us may require us to learn, study, or understand something new and different. God may give an idea that requires someone to go to school to learn to be an electrician to learn to connect wire to wire. God may give an idea that requires someone to learn plumbing to be able to fabricate what God has revealed. We must do what is necessary to work out with our hands the ideas that God releases to us, regardless of age or status in life. Some have the tendency of making God's ideas something religious. For example, God speaks to someone about how to change the world technologically; however, he says that God is sending him on mission to Africa, instead of working out and making technological breakthrough a reality. When someone responds this way, God will give the idea to someone else who will work it out with his hands. Our heads and our hands working together is key to operating in abundance. Any thinking man that doesn't want to use his hands is a man who will be rich in his head and poor in life. Any man who works with his hands and doesn't really think is a man who will be a slave to everyone else that produces. We tend to depend on everyone else, even though God has given us brilliant minds. Some have a gift of thinking, but their hands are lazy. Some have a capacity to pray, but their hands are lazy such that when God sends an idea, they don't catch it because they aren't thinking. When they do catch it, they turn it into a religion. Our hands don't want to work so it just stays in our head until someone else catches it.

> There's not one of us to whom God has not given an idea.

According to scripture, money is not our God but God gives us the power to get wealth, not of the miraculous or magical. We have had ideas that are now evident in our lives. God gives us these ideas as a way to prosper us financially and economically. Spirituality and economics are interrelated; thus, while we can discuss economics from a religious perspective and how we move in and out of power,

אתה

the reality is the people with money will make decisions on how things work. God is looking for his children to be come more economically savvy because things are shifting that way. The war we fight is a spiritual war tied directly to economics. If we're going to operate in abundance, we must start using these principles and teach the next generation to do the same. We must think and work with our hands. In scripture, God reminds us often of the hand of the Lord, especially in Exodus. This motif is found throughout scripture: ten fingers, ten principles of creation; ten fingers, ten Beatitudes; ten fingers, Ten Commandments; ten fingers, ten trials of Abraham; ten fingers, ten plagues of Egypt, which recognized that it was hand of the Lord that had come against them.

Miracles don't just happen because miracles are a work. This is what it means to work a miracle; that is, to do work. If someone causes miracles to happen, it means they have worked on it all night. The tabernacle of Moses was first an idea or blueprint that was released to someone's head; he used his hands to fabricate all the tools required to build it, even before Moses commanded it to be erected. The tabernacle did not descend out of heaven and appear for their immediate use; it had to be constructed. In our mystical movement, we were once waiting for things to manifest, but we were passively waiting. There are times when things manifest, but the biblical principle is that this kind of manifestation is a sign for what we're supposed to do. The sign is not final reality; it is a pointer to what we're capable of doing, and supposed to do. This is why they're called signs and wonders. If God brings down a car from heaven, it doesn't mean he wil continue to bring down cars from heaven. He brought down the car as a prototype that we learn to build it and manifest more of it on our own without God. Unbelievers, to a large measure, understand these principles; therefore, they can do certain things we cannot do.

While the unbeliever needs God for salvation, he doesn't need God to be able to create the technology. God has already created the technology. If God uses someone to produce something today and it's produced in righteousness, unbelievers can still take it and duplicate it. For example, China, without believing in our God, duplicates many American inventions. God has given all of us an idea; He hasn't exempted anyone. We may have lost it because we were waiting for something magical to ensue. We have to bring to fruition those ideas that God has given. We can start with a notebook, start drawing, start writing, start putting the ideas down. If we don't bring those ideas to fruition, someone else will.

אתה

Chapter 7

PSALM 23

> Consequently, we spend our whole lives trying to protect what we think is going to run out. And the measure and degree to which we have this thought, we have the same thought about God.

Ultimately, this means that we really don't believe in God, rather, we believe in ourselves because we really don't know God the way we think we do. If we really knew God, we would know that He never runs out. It's really very simple. Society, however, tell us that everything in the world is running out. Through various forms of media, we get the message that if we don't kill the next person to us to get what we want, it is going to run out. We have actually bought into that notion.

For example, we are told that the earth doesn't have any more land and we believe it, even though all human beings on earth today can fit into the state of Texas when standing side-by-side. We have been psychologically conditioned to believe and act as we are told; thus, we are huddled into cities and are made to step on each other to take what we want. This helps us to understand why the bible seems very "anti-city". The bible actually considers a city to be the presence of all kinds of evil where human beings are brought together to be controlled and not allowed to spread themselves upon the face of the earth. The first city on earth was built by Cain for his son, based on the blood of Abel whom Cain murdered. But God had commanded his people—Adam, Noah, and their children—to go east to spread out across the land and subdue it;

> So we will notice that all the things that God does is to show us that we are actually candidates and embodiments of the process of abundance.

OPERATING IN ABUNDANCE

אתה

notwithstanding, they huddled together to build a tower of confusion.

In scripture, Jerusalem was taken away. God took away Jerusalem that was on the earth because it had become a place of blood. Jeremiah, Ezekiel, and Isaiah said. So, He took away the Jerusalem of Israel and it became the city of the Jebusites, and a city of blood. which is an even bloodier city. We are examining our conditioning based in lack that is exacerbated by being told that we must live in cities where we are huddled together to step on and kill each other.

> Common sense is not so common

The city of Jerusalem wasn't destroyed because the foreigners were strong. Jerusalem was filled with blood from one end to the other. We gathered the people, made idols, and worshipped them. Again, God commanded them to spread out across the land in the east but they choose to huddle in cities in which many kinds of evils emerged and thrived.

Today, it seems that there is little to no criticism of cities. Even prophets, today, speak as if the cities were created by God. In fact, cities are human systems created for confusion and control. It seems that even people who live in cities think they are more civilized. The city is a place where barbarians live, hurt one another, and fight over crumbs, while there is plenty outside of the city. If we were living out in the desert and we each had a piece of land, we could grow our own food. Consider New York City, millions of people are compacted in its small subdivisions where they are stacked up on top of each other. There is enough land in the state of New York on which these people could live. Cities are not sustainable; consequently, in the next few years, people will actually go to live outside of cities but will enter them primarily for interaction. This doesn't mean that there are no good things about cities; however, many things someone can do in the city, he can do in the rural areas. People can scatter themselves and still do what they do in cities.

A major difference between rural areas and cities is villagers in rural areas don't generally murder each other. The crime rates are generally lower in rural areas compared to cities. From the vantage point of a city, someone would think there is not enough land, that the earth is shrinking. In fact, every human being on earth can have

אתה

two to three acres of land and the earth will still have enough land. This seems evident when we are flying in airplane. Looking out of an airplane window, we can see vast areas of unpopulated, open land. Not many areas are densely populated. This idea ofbeing huddled together in a city because it seems there is more safety and available resources is really what the Luciferians have done to humanity; this is not a conspiracy theory. They have convinced us that we cannot survive living alone somewhere in the mountains; that God is incapable of protecting us. They have convinced us that if we move away and outside of the city, we will die of hunger, even though all the food consumed in cities comes from outside the cities.

Every time human beings have done what we are doing now, God has come and scattered them. This is evident in scripture. We have no answer but it is important that we should not idolize the city. Children, who were born in cities, think the city is the place God wants us to be; however, there are enough resources in creation and enough space on earth for all of us (I flew across Asia and saw vasts lands when looking out of the airplane window). Consider China, there are billions of people in China most of whom are gathered in the different cities together. Consider the United States, someone can fly across the United States and see the amazing availability of land, even though certain groups of people want to take it, make it there own, and make everyone else beg them for it.

> God's fullness never runs out

It's a system that leads to the systematic enslavement of humanity, but we have lauded it as something great. It behooves us to look at these worldly structures with some skepticism. This is not about being against cities or suggesting that people should leave the cities. It is that cities take too much upon themselves to control everyone; we need to begin to think differently. There are enough resources on the face of the earth. If we mature to become who we are supposed to be in God, we can also help create more resources. On the other hand, if we focus on fighting over little things, operating in lack, we find ourselves not living in peace. All wars are fought over resources; one person convinces another person that there is not enough available. So, they are ready to die to get it.

אתה

Once, they convinced us that gold was running out. All of sudden, they told us they had discovered even more gold than ever before. We have to think from this perspective—there is more available than ever before—and apply it to our personal lives. We must ask ourselves from where we operate: the position of lack or the position of abundance. Our answer determines our psychological well-being. David said, "I operate from the position of abundance, from the position that God is shepherd, full of blessing, and He release it towards me." All the things that God does is to show us that we are actually candidates and embodiments of the process of abundance.

Psalm 23:6, "Surely goodness and mercy shall follow me all the days of my life."

Surely	אַךְ (ach)
Goodness	טוֹב (to·vv)
And mercy	וָחֶסֶד (va·che·sed)
Will follow me	יִרְדְּפוּנִי (yir·de·fu·ni)
All the days of my life	כָּל־יְמֵי חַיָּי (kol yemei chayah)

> God himself is the goodness.

This text is structured with the first word comprising of the first letters of the names of the fathers of Israel—Abraham, Isaac, and Jacob. The word "ach" becomes Aleph Yod Yod, which is Abraham, Yitzchak, Yaakov. God said, "I am the God of Abraham," in Exodus 3:6, and that this will be His name forever. Jesus repeated this declaration in Matthew 22:32. In Jewish tradition, Abraham is considered to be the carrier of mercy. Now when David said "Surely goodness and mercy shall follow me all the days of my life," we know that he is referring to God's goodness

אתה

and God's mercy, two key aspects of His nature. However, when Israelites pray, they say "the mercies of Abraham" which is considered the ever-flowing river from heaven that flows into their hearts. It's a reference to God's nature flowing through the patriarch Abraham and his seed, Isaac and Jacob. Israel is actually the recipient of mercy; God said to Abraham that He would have mercy on them and cause His goodness to pass before them (Exodus 33:19). God does this continuously. The way this worked for David was a genetic channel whereby God was constantly following him. For us, it works through the Son of God, Jesus Christ, who carries the goodness and the mercy of God.

> Goodness cannot germinate where someone is not willing to die.

The gematria of ach (אִיּ) is 21. Two plus one is three, which is not only the number of God but also the number of the ancestors of Israel. So when a Jew says Abraham, Isaac, and Jacob, they are actually referring to God because it is the name that God took for himself. He's the God of Abraham Isaac and Jacob.

Tovv is the word for goodness and its gematria is eight. Tovv begins with Tet. Tet has a numerical value of nine, which is also the number for death. In the Zohar, when the letters came to God to explain why they should be the first letter in the AlephBet, Tet came to God and said he should be the first one because he was the beginning of Tovv. But God also became death. Now, if we think about goodness, we will notice that, according to scripture, goodness flows from the capacity to die. Jesus said in John 12:24:

> "Verily, verily, I say unto you, Except a corn of wheat fall into the ground and die, it abideth alone: but if it die, it bringeth forth much fruit." (KJV)

The idea of goodness, as connected to death, is not about complete demise and disappearing. This death is the constant dying to oneself that allows goodness to germinate. Goodness cannot germinate where someone is not willing to die. Every act of goodness suppresses something else that is evil. In other words, every time we do something good, something in us dies that is contrary to that nature of God. Paul revealed this when he wrote, "I die daily" (1 Corinthians 15:31). Paul died by constantly doing something good. In Jewish terms, constantly doing mitzvahs demonstrates God's goodness. Usually, when we want to do something really good, we encounter doubt; we weigh the pro and cons of it. We consider our own needs, own position, and the cost to us; however, if we do the good act, we've killed something. At the very least, we begin to kill the mindset of operating from lack. And out of that death, goodness germinates. We don't have to find another way to crucify ourselves because doing good is crucifixion. Sharing kindness with someone who doesn't deserve it is a crucifixion, without having to go through the pain of understanding what one is doing in the process of crucifixion.

> There's no end to the believer's abundance.

The next word is mercy or "chesed" (חֶסֶד). The first letter is Chet (חֶ) which has a numerical value of 8. The Hebrew symbol for Chet is pictured as a closed door, which is impassable unless we are initiated. The Hebrew symbol for Chet is very similar to the symbol for Heh (ה); however, The Heh symbol is pictured as a hinged door because of how the Dalet (ד) and the Vav (ו) combine. Chet is a closed door. In the mystery realm, to crossover through the door of Chet, we must die, which is an initiation into the mysteries, not physical death. Thus, Chet is the door that is in front of someone who is not initiated. The person who would enter the closed door needs mercy. We cannot enter unless we are prayed in mercy.

Eight is the numerical value and the gematria of Chet and Tovv, respectively. This indicates that God's goodness becomes real in our lives and is better understood when we are initiated in the mysteries of God. Without our initiation in the mysteries of God, we usually take God's goodness for granted and we won't understand that His goodness brings the mysteries of heaven into our lives. Romans 2:4 says,

> Or do you despise the riches of His goodness, forbearance,
> and longsuffering, not knowing that the goodness of
> God leads you to repentance? (NKJV)

Repentance is one of the principles for initiation into the mystery

אתה

of the nature of God because without it we cannot enter. Thus, David revealed that being followed by goodness is the constant opportunity for initiation into the mystery of divinity. The mystery of God has to do with the fullness of God and his infinite supply; He never runs out of anything. The simple mystery is if we are in God, we are complete because goodness is not just something God has; God himself is the goodness.

The initiation of a believer into the goodness of God is an initiation into the very nature of God Himself. When we stand before a good act that we are supposed to do, we're standing before a door of the mystery of initiation. Every time we are called to do something great and good, we are standing before a closed door. Only the act of goodness can open it. We are standing in front of an initiatory process into an aspect of divinity. Every day and every moment, God gives us opportunities to be initiated into a dimension of His being by bringing dysfunctional people into our lives whom we're supposed to help or by making our families dysfunctional enough so we can help them. He comes in different ways so that we understand this. Because of the interest of God in our lives and the vastness of His divinity, He is always making space and putting a door in front of us to initiate us into a mystery of an aspect of His being.

> God is constantly removing that which is a hindrance between you and Him by the blood of his Son to make sure that you have constant access to the fullness of your Father in heaven.

The word that is translated "follow" is "yirdefuni" (יִרְדְּפוּנִי) and its gematria is 360. This number is a reference to going full circle. David was saying that goodness and mercy will follow me and initiate me into the mysteries of the nature of God and the mystery of the fullness of creation. Therefore, if we operate in the fullness of who God is and his abundance, we're always brought to a place of the fullness of creation. We're brought to the full circle, which is comprised of His never-ending goodness and mercy.

Each time we move into a position of lack, we can restart the principle that causes the inflow of divine plentitude into our lives. By

OPERATING IN ABUNDANCE

אתה

returning to the process of creation in Genesis 1 on the sixth day, and by operating in abundance, we can always go full circle. We must recognize that goodness and mercy pursue us. We are not chasing after them. They are behind us not in front of us. They chase after us because fullness and abundance are overflowing principles of God. He is eager to break open the door so that we can be inundated with all that God has in store for us. The 360 gematria of "follow" signifies that this overflow is all around us all the day of our lives.

> God blesses you because He's God and because you believe that He will bless you.

We live in the world that informs our mindsets of lack whereby we tend to think that God created the earth to run out. Our reality is that we can constantly return to Him who is the fullness of everything. God sends His goodness and mercy, Himself, to be available at the point of our need. Every time we run out, goodness and mercy meet to create an arc to manifest the vision of what is coming from the realm of divinity into our lives. In other words, we never really run out, except in our heads. If we are children of God, our first task, when we are inclined to operate in lack, is to turn ourselves toward God; His fullness never runs out.

The last words of "all the days of my life" is yemey khayay (חַיָּיְמֵיכֹּל). Yemey is spelled Yod Mem Yod and has a numerical value of 60, which is the number of creation. This is about returning to the point of the creation of man and using the principles of creation to reformulate, rectify, reenergize, re-scroll, and redirect our lives. The gematria of "khayay" equals ten: Chet (8), Yod (10), Yod (10) equals 28. Two plus eight equals ten. Psalm 23 begins with the number 3, which can represent Abraham, Isaac, and Jacob. It ends with the number 10, the principle of creation. David was saying that he operated in the fullness of the promise that was made to Abraham, Isaac, and Jacob. He operated as a person who constantly stood in the presence of the door of divine mystery. The door is closed, but we always have access because of what is behind us—goodness and mercy.

Thus, we have access to the door of divine mystery; however, not

אתה

everyone who comes to the door is initiated because for them the door is closed. Anyone who comes to this door but doesn't know the God of Abraham, Isaac, and Jacob can't access anything. Goodness and mercy that follow behind us is what determines our future because whatever we place behind us, we will harvest in the future. Our future is being pushed towards us by that which stands behind us. Because God doesn't want anything behind us but Himself, He makes it a constant duty to forgive us. God doesn't want anything else chasing us but Him. When David sinned, He didn't say, "Oh my goodness! All my sins are following me! What am I going to do? Instead, he said, "Surely, goodness and mercy are chasing me." This was every moment of his life. Further, David said they will purse him all the days of his life. In fact, they are pursuing him even into the grave. If goodness and mercy pursue us all the days of our lives and our lives don't truly end after death, then they pursue us all the way to the next world. When believers die in this world, they don't leave to go to the dirt; they go to a new life.

God follows us even into the grave. On the other side of the realm, God's goodness and mercy continue to chase us because they pursue us eternally. God's goodness and mercy—demonstrated through Abraham, Isaac, and Jacob—is still alive and constantly chasing their descendants. Jesus intimated this truth when he expressed that God is not a God of the dead but the God of the living (Luke 20:38). This chasing allows the believer to start again; there is no end to the believer's abundance.

Even though the truth is there it is no end to our abundance, we are inclined to say that there is an end to abundance; therefore, we continue to operate in lack. We think we don't have enough, so we don't give. We worry about what will happen to us, so we don't move towards meeting other's needs. We don't think from the perspective of the flow of abundance. We believe we never have enough to be able to do anything for anyone else until we can provide for ourselves.

Dalet represents an open door with the hinges on it, whereas the letter Chet represents a closed Dalet. This symbolism is seen in the self-affirmation of Jesus when he said, "I am the door" (John 10:9). Many of the themes in Psalm 23 are evident in Gospel of John: "I'm the good Shepherd; I came that they might have life and have it more abundantly; I am the door by me the Sheep go in an out and find pasture. David was telling us Psalm 23 should be the anthem of the believer.

When I first became a Christian, every church I went to would recite two prayers: "Our 'Father who art in heaven" and "the Lord is my shepherd." Until the Lord told me to teach Psalm 23, I didn't realize that it should be our mantra. God is the embodiment of over abundance, overflowing abundance, hyper abundance, and supernatural abundance!

He tell us, "I carry this and I pursue you with it. When you put a block between me and you, I use the blood of my son take it away so that I can always have access to pour it upon you. I want to bless you. I want to fill you with my goodness. I don't have any problems that inhibit me from blessing you. Surely goodness and mercy shall follow you all the days of your life—both your earthly and eternal existence."

We—those who know God operating in our lives the way Adam operated in the garden—are the focus. God's intention for us, as his children, is to bring us constantly to the position of the full supply that Adam had in the garden where there was no sin and no lack. Being born from above is the way God restores this to us. If our sin remains a problem, then Jesus died in vain. All we need to do is to go Him, to his blood. By the blood of his son, God is constantly removing that which is a hindrance between Him and us to make sure that we have constant access to the fullness of our Father in Heaven. There's nothing between God and us that is holding us back right now. Operating from the place of the full supply of the father's heart for us is an incredible life. God continues to pursue us to manifest the fullness of who He is. Amen.

Jesus told us He is the door, and the good shepherd who feeds the sheep and the lambs. He told us that he came that we might have life and have it more abundantly; He is the door we can go in and out of to find pasture. If our reason for God not blessing us is our shortcomings, then we must explain the reason He is blessing the unbeliever. We must abandoned that kind of thinking. Walking righteously is still important, but it isn't the reason God blesses us. God blesses us because He's God and because we believe that He will bless us. The Bible says, "Without faith, it's impossible to please God", not "With or without sin, it's

אתה

impossible to please God" (Hebrews 11:6). In this scripture, God uses faith purposely because it is by faith we are forgiven, healed, and have access to God. Faith is the person of Christ Jesus. He is that door we can't run away from. We can operate in abundance if we understand this everytime we do something good. Every time we believe God, we are opening a door—a door of mystery. The door follows us everywhere. We don't have to seek for the door; it pursues and follow us. It is the door of goodness and mercy. Amen.

Appendix A: The Hebrew Aleph Bet

Letter	Name	Numerical Value
א	Aleph	1
ב	Bet	2
ג	Gimel	3
ד	Dalet	4
ה	Heh	5
ו	Vav	6
ז	Zayin	7
ח	Chet	8
ט	Tet	9
י	Yod	10
כ	Kaph	20
ל	Lamed	30
מ	Mem	40
נ	Nun	50
ס	Samech	60
ע	Ayin	70
פ	Pay	80
צ	Tsade	90
ק	Qoph	100
ר	Resh	200
ש	Shin	300
ת	Tav	400

אתה

ABOUT THE AUTHOR

Adonijah Okechukwu Ogbonnaya (BA, MATS, MA, Ph.D) is the founder of AACTEV8 International, an Apostolic and Kingdom Ministry which works with the Body of Christ across the globe for Soul Winning, Discipleship, Training, and Equipping the saints in Kingdom mysteries and Kingdom living. Located in Venice, California, Dr. Ogbonnaya (also known as A. Okechukwu or "Dr. O") began preaching the Word of God in the 1970s in his teenage years. He has served as a missionary, church planter, pastor, and professor. Dr. Ogbonnaya has traveled and ministered in over 25 nations in Asia, Africa, Europe, and North and South America with the message of the Gospel of Jesus Christ. He has seen God perform various signs and wonders as He promised in Mark 16:1–17—the blind receive sight, the deaf hear, the lame walk, the dead are raised, the barren receive the fruit of the womb, lives are transformed and minds renewed. He has focused on helping believers engage the spiritual realities which have been opened up for them in the person of the Lord Jesus Christ. He is a Hebrew-born native of Nigeria, West Africa. He earned his Ph.D and Master's degree in theology and personality and his Master's in religion from Claremont School of Theology. He completed his M.A. in theological studies at Western Evangelical Seminary and his B.A. in religion at Hillcrest Christian College in Canada. He also holds a Ph.D in business publishing.

He is also the presenter of numerous teachings found at: www.aactev8.com.

Dr. Ogbonnaya is married to Pastor Benedicta and is blessed with four wonderful children and grandchildren.

SeraphCreative
Heaven's Heart for Earth

Seraph Creative is a collective of artists, writers, theologians & illustrators who desire to see the body of Christ grow into full maturity, walking in their inheritance as Sons Of God on the Earth.

Sign up to our newsletter to know about the release of the next book in the series, as well as other exciting releases.

Visit our website :
www.seraphcreative.org

Printed in Great Britain
by Amazon